Perennial Love

Arun Berry & Pradeep Berry

Perennial Love by Arun Berry & Pradeep Berry

This book is written to provide information and motivation to readers. Its purpose is not to render any type of psychological, legal, or professional advice of any kind. The content is the sole opinion and expression of the author, and not necessarily that of the publisher.

Copyright © 2022 by Arun Berry & Pradeep Berry

All rights reserved. No part of this book may be reproduced, transmitted, or distributed in any form by any means, including, but not limited to, recording, photocopying, or taking screenshots of parts of the book, without prior written permission from the author or the publisher. Brief quotations for noncommercial purposes, such as book reviews, permitted by Fair Use of the U.S. Copyright Law, are allowed without written permissions, as long as such quotations do not cause damage to the book's commercial value.

ISBN: 978-1-951670-48-1 (Paperback)
ISBN: 978-1-951670-49-8 (Digital)

Printed in the United States of America.

Contents

Key Takeaways from Arun and Shobha's Story	13
Authors' Note for the Readers	19
Authors' Viewpoint on Life and Happiness	50
Death of a Shuagan Shobha Berry	55
Preface and Authors' Note	57
Our Childhood	59
Philosophy of Happiness and Life Partners in our Lifetime	62
Biological Brothers	64
The Life of the Authors	67
Tributes to Shobha Berry	70
Our Wonderful Family	72
Shobha Berry – A Wonderful Wife	74
Pradeep's Wife, Connie	77
Harrowing Childhood Memoirs	79
Marriage is Wonderful	81
Beginning of our Love – Arun and Shobha	83
Another Player in our Lives	85
Childhood Life	86
Shobha's Children	88

SHOBHA WAS THE ULTIMATE	89
SHOBHA IN USA AND ENGLAND	91
SHOBHA AND ARUN BERRY	93
SHOBHA AND HER KITCHEN	95
SHOBHA AND HER HEALTH	96
STAYING WITH HER BODY	97
OUR WONDERFUL SISTER'S VIEWS	98
ARUN, THE CLASSICAL SINGER	99
LIFE IS A DUTY	100
WE ARE BORN WITH PURPOSE	101
EDUCATION IS WEALTH	102
DEATH AND FACE	104

The love of a wife is a worthwhile experience for our lives—and it is especially true for Arun and Pradeep Berry. We are excited to have the opportunity to go beyond our own lives and let the world know our story. We want everyone to know—your marriage is the best; even though you may have problems, you just have to solve them!

Please follow our guide for a happy, healthy, loving life in your marriage. You will find worthwhile answers for your problems in life—be it parents or children or any other family member. Trust your ears and brain to find an answer—you won't be disappointed with your own decision to make the best of relationships with others—especially your wife.

Don't forget that your wife is your best friend as well as your soulmate. Give her your love and happiness to the maximum to keep a wonderful marriage. Different people have different lifestyles, but creative people make their world full of love and happiness. Your wife is your asset in your old ages—but people don't realize this until it's very late. One can learn from the Malthusian theory of the 1920s that decreed—time and tide wait for none!

Arun Berry graduated from Hindu College, while Pradeep did his education from Shri Ram College of Commerce, affiliated with the University of Delhi. Both of us did our post-graduation from Delhi University and were happily married to our respective wives.

We were responsible for our destiny and our own lives in a world of competition and ups and downs. Love was and still is the best thing we have ever had in our lives.

Happiness and suffering are the root cause of the human race, and even animals can be your friends and sometimes your enemies—depending on how you treat them.

Arun's younger son Ashish got a small dog from our brother Vikram when they lived in Rohini, Delhi. Ashish named him Jimmy. When Jimmy got big, he turned into a ferocious, big dog that scared everyone and was very protective of his family as a police commissioner. He would watch the family and could immediately smell those family members not worthy of being liked. Dogs can smell a bad person, and now we realize how smart Jimmy was.

Jimmy was instrumental in protecting us and was a very important part of our lives. While Arun and his family were moving from their first house in Bali Nagar to the current house in Rohini, Pradeep was slightly concerned about the safety of moving to the second house. However, having an excellent dog-like Jimmy was a wonderful gift to Arun and his family.

When both brothers went to Vaishno Devi Temple in Jammu to pay homage to Vaishno Devi, Arun's son Ashish and his family looked after Jimmy. Shobha, too was very fond of Jimmy. Jimmy was wonderful and very happy to see Pradeep and Connie whenever they came to India.

When Pradeep and Connie Berry visited Arun and his family in Rohini, Jimmy was very nice to Connie. Jimmy was very aggressive and was given special dog care for six days. Connie was not very happy about it, but it was necessary to keep him away from the guests staying in the house. Pradeep says Connie was very upset to see Jimmy looking pale and depressed after returning to Arun and Shobha's house, which upset all the family members.

Later, Shobha was very happy with Jimmy, and her love for the dog was worth watching. She was very happy to be with Jimmy and treated him as a part of her family. She would feed him like a child or like her own son, and it was very nice to see Jimmy eating, playing, and sleeping in her arms. Shobha was extremely upset and angry when Jimmy suddenly died due to a heart problem. His death was very difficult for Shobha to handle, and she often wept and cried. It was very upsetting for her.

Thanks, Shobha Berry, for loving a very good animal and a great family friend. Arun and Shobha were dedicated to their dog Jimmy—their darling.

It is not easy to understand the humanity of animals and how animals can be your best friend—especially when you are in trouble. They can do anything to protect their own master, regardless of whether you are rich, poor, old, or young. They give you unconditional love and happiness for taking care of them. An excellent description of this love was the relation of Arun and Shobha with Zimmy.

Now, things are different than before, and we're going through the crisis of missing our wives. Love is beautiful and soothing in our lives. So please don't forget to send a message of love to your family and friends, and even your neighbors and university.

Allow us to share more—one can digest in discussing the world of love and happiness no matter what and who it is. Even if a smile comes across a person's face, it is a blessing for us.

Don't forget that one day, you may need a smile—so why not give a smile and get a smile?

This book is a tribute to the once-in-a-lifetime love story between Arun Berry and his late beloved wife, Shobha. Many times in life, the decisions we make shape our future—whether we are consciously aware of it or not. For Arun Berry, the decision to meet Shobha Khanna with her parents in Bengali Market, New Delhi, India, would be the defining moment of his life. Although he was hesitant, shy, and insecure, with many uncomfortable memories, once he met her, he realized that she would be his future life partner—he was convinced it was destiny.

With his future wife Shobha, Arun would soon come to discover a new life—a life full of love, memorable experiences, a supportive family, and excellent career opportunities. She, too, was very happy to find a handsome husband of her own choice. It was a wonderful gift from the Khanna family to give their daughter in marriage to Arun, and the two were later wed in 1972. It was the start of a happy marriage that would still be flourishing were it not for Shobha's unexpected demise in 2018—leaving Arun at a crossroads of his own.

Who is Arun Berry?

Arun K. Berry has worked as a senior manager in the pharmaceutical industry for decades. In his long and fruitful career, Berry conducted thousands of viability studies for pharmaceutical drugs to determine if certain medications are good for the human body.

Berry takes pride in being an expert in handling the turnaround of sick patients with his own long-term medical experience in pharmaceuticals. Berry credits his career success to his late wife of 48 years, Shobha, who passed away in 2018.

In light of Shobha's passing, Arun faced intense grief and even authored a book to immortalize her memory. Nowadays, the author spends time with his family—two sons, a daughter-in-law, and two granddaughters—who share his pain and loss. His younger brother Pradeep Berry shared this, who unexpectedly lost his American-born wife of 44 years in 2015. Both brothers thus decided to share their wonderful thoughts on Shobha.

Why this story?

People fall in 'love' all the time. But true love is rare. That's what makes this story incredibly valuable. Arun Berry, an educated young man from India, met a lovely lady at the behest of his family in Delhi and instantly fell in love. Over the next four decades, the couple stood by each other and lived a special life, guided by true love.

In Arun's book, the author shares his lessons from this magical union and explores his journey from a timid man to a seasoned marketing manager, which was possible because of Shobha's influence.

Pure Love, a Gift from God

A collection of carefully woven and pure love stories based upon a true story of love and sad chapters of life. Each chapter of love, a wonderful gift and a very strong waterfall of humanity and kindness towards others- before and after an emotional setback and lack of happiness in his own lives, however, he is very happy helping others in memory of his wonderful wife, Mrs. Berry or his Wife Shobha or Shobha Berry.

Hospital to Earth

Who would cry for you or me?? It's a wonderful true story of true love between a beautiful young educated girl from a wealthy family in Delhi, India. The future generations of her family life were predictable in her own life when she was born in Delhi, India. It was miss Shobha Khanna from a wealthy family in Delhi, India. A teaching young girl, and God wanted her to marry a Delhi-born boy, a B. A Honours from Hindu College in Delhi University and a Lawyer in Delhi, India, and a senior Medical professional.

Arun Berry never thought about moving to Bali Nagar and then to the west of Delhi to Rohni, Delhi, India. He is the best seller of crying and crying in his crushed life. It is very painful for him to understand that his wife, Mrs. Shobha Berry, was born in Delhi, India, as Miss Shobha Khanna's daughter of Mr. and Mrs. KL Khanna and Mrs. Santosh Khanna. She would be gone after 46 years of our marriage life.

Do I need to laugh or cry for my loss of losing my wonderful wife, Shobha.

A riveting story of true love and ambition, the thirst and happiness for success in life after suffering from the lord of darkness in early childhood, and happiness was looking forward to a better life and career advancement. Meanwhile, the obsession lured, bidding its own life and its time eliminating a new wave of happiness that gets in its way to discuss future life, until it got whatever it was craving for and that was the best part of my life when I got my life with my wife Shobha Khanna my first and last love, Mrs. Shobha Berry on June 25, 1972, until her demise on November 8, 2018.

Shobha and Arun Berry, two bodies and one soul, after 46 years of our marriage and granddaughters and two boys, are truly suffering from the lord of darkness in your memories. However, at the same time, we both were very unhappy with the demise of our Family members. Mrs. Connie Berry, wife of your brother-in-law Pradeep

Berry lost his wonderful wife, Connie, on February 28, 2015. All our family life has taken a very big toll on losing our dear ones.

Shobha, please call me by your thoughts and kindness of voice, as my life is truly very happy with your memories and blessings for your life. I would never burn like a half Lamp in the Air or the lord of darkness. I am very unhappy thinking about our life when we both were very happy with each other's thoughts and prayers. Finally, we got married on a very special day of June 25, 1972. I was very happy sitting on the decorated Horse with a beautiful smile and a beautiful shining hat and a nephew behind my back on the horse- an old family tradition of Indian culture. It is very difficult for me to explain why I am not very happy with being in my dreams of your memories and blessings to our family and friends, especially to your children and granddaughters and your brother-in-law Pradeep Berry, my younger biological brother. Our late sister Mrs. Kiran Revri and now her husband, Surinder Revri, also left us to heaven before her death and yours. Our Connie darling, our family, too, died on February 28, 2015, in the USA. Pradeep was very unhappy and was suffering from the lord of darkness and crushing death of his life partner Connie.

Please let me write you the Routing on the wall that you would never be forgotten and remain in our hearts and souls. I am still hiding everywhere from your life in my own heart and happiness.

There is no life without a woman, no matter what and how you believe?? However, realize when you are truly unhappy thinking about your mother and your mother and father. Especially the mother- she is the mother who kept you nine months in her own body and the lord of darkness without your mother. Your wife is an important part of your life and happiness and prosperity in your life and your thoughts

We all ask goddess Durga Mata the Laxmi, Vaishnow Devi Laxmi maa, Kali Maa ka mandir in Delhi, Parvati, Gauri, and your biological wife have a strong bond and happiness when you are traveling in the lord to bless our family in the world. However, the only thing that we both are very lucky to have our wife' Shobha Berry, and Mrs. Constance Ann Berry of husband Pradeep Berry, and Shobha was for Arun Berry.

Till we have a wonderful gift to leave for humanity and kindness towards others, we would be very much remembered in the world or even in the books. However, if we don't do that, no one would even believe our existence on the earth.

Arun Berry and Pradeep Berry

Love wins Sun, Moon, Stars, Sky, Ocean, Lord, and it's water and earth. In reality, love wins the world and its wonderful people and the citizens who have been in the lord of darkness and happiness and prosperity. Love is lord. Love is a very strong relationship between humanity and kindness to others, especially for the family of humanity.

Key Takeaways from Arun and Shobha's Story

In Arun Berry's love story with Shobha, we learn a few key life lessons:

- **You Are Your Decisions**—The decision to marry each other made Arun and Shobha's destiny a wonderful gift to both of them—similar to his biological brother Pradeep Berry and his wife Connie Berry in the USA.

The same thing can be said of their wonderful sister Kiran Revri, who had a happy life with her husband and children. Her death in 2019 caused a big loss in the lives of the brothers. Death is a historic moment in everybody's lives, but the gravity of the loss differs from individual to individual based upon the intensity of their love for each other.

- **Reading for Mental Nourishment**—Arun Berry learned from his beloved Shobha the value of social life. Shobha would spend four to six hours watching different episodes of life each day.

This culture of reading helped the two authors narrate their emotional days in this powerful book. The culture of watching TV and TV serials and episodes was very helpful for Arun to think about writing on social issues. By learning more about our areas of interest, we stimulated our intelligence and unlocked numerous growth activities. This key lesson both of them learned from their spouses.

- **Make Good Use of Your Time**—Arun and Shobha made the best social life and happiness in their lives.

- **Making a Marriage**—This is perhaps the most pronounced lesson we can all learn from the couple's utter dedication and love. Arun loved and treasured his Shobha throughout. From the start, they got married without the objections of any family members. They stuck together and became each other's best friends.

This commitment and attitude are what made their marriage stick together like glue for more than 48 years. Every couple, young or old, can learn a lot on how to make a marriage work.

- **Courage in the Face of Loss**—This is another key lesson that we can learn. When Arun lost Shobha, he was more than devastated. He couldn't sleep or eat. It took a lot of courage for him to get back up again. He took to praying to God to cherish the memory of his beloved Shobha. He talked about their story as much as he could and treasured her memory wherever he went. Indeed, Arun showed tremendous courage and loyalty in the face of such a tragic loss. The author says that true love can be a double-edged sword in the face of loss. But with courage and by cherishing all the memorable experiences, we can gradually rise from the darkness of loss.

Books

Arun Berry has co-authored this book along with his brother Pradeep Berry. They explore the authors' shared life experiences, careers, marriages, struggles, and eventually the tragic losses that ended it all.

Arun and Pradeep's first book celebrates Arun's true and special bond and his beloved wife, Shobha. It is a love story brewed in classic Indian family-style and sealed through marriage in 1972.

The book shows that true love is possible and in a very special way. The author details how he met Shobha and fell in love with her and vice versa. At the same time, Pradeep explores his experiences in the US, his decades of steadfast, loving union with Connie, and ultimately the unbearable pain and suffering upon her demise.

This wonderful book is also a tribute to their sister Kiran Revri, who also passed away recently.

"Two bodies with one soul"

Before starting this biography of our true love, I have to give my highest tribute to my Shobha because of the immortal love she gave me—a love that will remain evergreen and lifelong. With valuable messages about the nature of love, this book creates the true love, hope, and faith we shared. Imagining this destiny and love is the only comfort I have left. I had never realized how life could be changed by love, and through my devotion to fulfilling Shobha's desires, I am sure God would fulfill both my wish and hers. Perhaps it was a difficult test of life—an exam we had to face to pass again with a gold medal for our love to last in the next life. In this book, I examine how destiny and love have shaped the course of my life. It is extremely important to mention that Shobha's demise was the most painful event of my life and is in my mind every moment—day and night. When I go to bed when I dream and get up, it remains with me—thoughts of pain wander in my brain. I feel like I am dreaming, but then I wake up, and I start to think so much. Now, things are very difficult, and I am not a very happy peon.

We must mention that Shobha was a very great fan of social networking. Later in life, when her legs were getting worse due to her vascular surgery, she was a super successful TV and Facebook expert; she knew all the Bollywood and Hollywood movies and would watch all the TV episodes in her family room in the evening and night. Her knowledge was wonderful, and her memory was good to suggest what we see in movies or TV shows, and what TV programs were worth seeing and what not. Her advice was a magnificent gift to our family and friends and her brother-in-law Pradeep. It is amazing how Shobha became instrumental in giving her suggestions on what to watch.

Shobha always wanted her brother-in-law Pradeep to call her from the USA—especially when Pradeep and Connie stayed in Sanibel Island and Marco Island in Florida, where they escaped from the cold weather in Evanston every year from January to March. Shobha, Connie, and Pradeep were very happy to talk to her over the cellphone about the water, beach, ocean, and dinner. She would love to see her brother-in-law Pradeep be happy.

Since 2015, this is not possible—ever since Connie's untimely death, Pradeep hasn't gone. Shobha is gone, too, leaving us on November 8, 2018.

Authors' Note for the Readers

> *Love is beautiful, especially if it's a true love granted by God and a wonderful gift on the planet.*
>
> By Arun and Pradeep Berry

BOTH SHOBHA AND Arun were obsessed with each other, and so were Connie and Pradeep. The two brothers loved their one and only sister Kiran Revri till her death on December 20, 2019.

Arun Berry is the eldest son of late Lala Ram Parshad Berry and Shanti Berry ('Shanti mummy'), who died when Arun and his brother Pradeep were 11 months and

2 months old, respectively. It was even more difficult when Ram Parshad Berry married Shanti's younger sister Kanta ('Kanta mummy'), who died after five years, leaving behind a baby girl only one hour old—Rita Berry or Pappi (known as Kiran Revri after her marriage).

Ram Parshad Berry married a third time Satya Malhotra, an outsider from another family. Satya became Uma Berry, who wanted her children Sunil and Vikram to be raised in the family.

Arun and Pradeep were raised by their paternal grandparent Lala Durga Parshad Berry's family, while the baby Rita was raised by our maternal grandparent Shri Ishwar Dass Mehra, the father of seven daughters and two boys, including our Shanti and Kanta mummy.

We three were raised jointly by both our grandparents. Ram Parshad was a great moral support to the three of them, especially since Arun and Pradeep lived separately from their sister.

Both the brothers finished high school, college, and postgraduate education from the top colleges of Delhi University. It was a great blessing to both of us in our Berry family—no doubt we both had our Shanti mummy's genes to be educated in our whole family at that time until one of our nephews became educated. Going forward, time would tell, as family wealth was a stopping point for those generations to avoid schooling and perhaps education, Arun and Pradeep both are self-made first generations of the Berry family heritage—no doubt about that. Not bragging, but these are the facts. We got our education, while others got our grandfathers' wealth. A balanced game between education and wealth?

God took our wonderful mothers but gave us the wonderful gift of happiness—education and an advanced career in our professions in the corporate sector. We must remember our success through our hard and smart work.

The death of our paternal grandparents in 1969 was a big blow to both Arun and Pradeep Berry. Their sister Rita got married to Surinder Revri that year.

Arun Berry was introduced to Shobha Khanna by his extended family. They both fell in love and got married on June 25, 1972. Their son Ashiem Berry was born in 1975.

Young Pradeep left for the USA in 1976 with just seven dollars and met Constance Ann Fuller on January 24, 1976. It was love at first sight, which took them to a Chicago courtroom days later, culminating in secret love marriage.

Our Massi ji Sudesh massi and Dilbagh uncle from Raipur.

She was a wonderful classical singer in India from 1969 till 2017. She was the first girl in Delhi to receive the gold medal from the Sangeet Academy, presented by the first President of India—Rajendra Prasad. She was a composer and singer of bhajans, thumri, and Punjabi geet and was a teacher at Modern School, Delhi, and Sardar Patel Mahavidalya. She sang at All India Radio Station in Delhi, India, and was one of the top singers.

She taught Arun and Pradeep classical music from 1961 to 1963 and later. She wanted to remain unmarried, but our old-fashioned values were raised to get her married to a wonderful husband, the late Shri Dilbagh Rai Ahuja from Bhilai. Later, they moved to Raipur, Madhya Parsdesh—now in Chattisgarh.

Shri Sudesh Ahuja was our wonderful biological aunt. She was known as Lata Behen and called Sima Ahuja by her husband, the late Shri Dilbagh Rai Ahuja, who worked in Bhilai and later in Raipur. Sudesh or Sima was a very popular classical singer and a wonderful TV singer from 1963 to 2017. Now both have died. Sudesh aunty took care of Arun, Pradeep, and our sister Rita. She was extremely well respected in the classical music industry in India and was the biological sister of our late mothers Shanti Berry and Kanta Berry. The first Indian President, Dr. Rajendra Prasad, Sudesh, was even invited to the Rashtrapati Bhavan or President's House for singing, especially when Dr. Prasad was sick and wanted her to sing devotional ragas. Her face resembled our biological mother, Shanti Berry

Thanks to massi ji for taking care of Arun, Pradeep, and sister Rita.

"You are never too old to set another goal or to dream a new dream."

— C.S. Lewis

My Shobha

This is the true story of Arun Berry, whose wife Shobha's demise called for this book to be written. At the same time, Arun's younger biological brother, Pradeep Berry, also wrote four books in memory of his wife Constance Ann Berry, Ph.D., a Professor of Spanish, German, and French. Also, this book reflects on the death of our sister Kiran Revri, whose demise on December 20, 2019, became an integral part of this book. These three women were wonderful gifts of God to us, who taught us how to love and care for the Lord, embody humanity, donate to charities, and help others in need of help. They were the most important part of our lives.

Connie and Pradeep especially flew to Delhi in January 1994 to celebrate the marriage of Priya Revri—daughter of our late sister Kiran Revri—to Dev Makkar in Delhi, India. Since it was very cold, Connie and Pradeep went on a wonderful trip to the Palace on Wheels Delhi to Rajastan-Jaipur-Jaisalmer-Udaipur-Bikaner-Agra-Jodhpur. After the trip, we were very happy to participate in Priya and Dev's marriage rituals along with Arun, Shobha, and the family.

It was very nice to have wonderful memories of those days. At that time, Arun and Shobha were residing in C38 Bali Nagar, Delhi. Another trip Connie and Pradeep made was in 2004. That was the last time Connie was in India, and that was very painful to me, whereas I was going every year to India except in 2012- 2014 when Connie was suffering from the darkness of second cancer. February 2004 was also the trip when Pradeep met Priyanka Gandhi and Rahul Gandhi at Vaishno Devi.

Ashish Berry married Mona Gulati in 2005. Today, Arun, Ashiem, Ashish, Mona, and their daughters Krishana and Radhika Berry live in the Rohini house, where Pradeep occasionally goes and stays whenever he comes from the USA.

Shobha was present at the time when everyone was coming to see Arun, Shobha, Pradeep, Connie, Surinder And Pappi and all our relations at Bali Nagar, before moving from Katra Neel and after Bali Nagar in Rohini's, where Arun lives with Ashiem, Ashish, his wife Mona, Daughters Krishana and Radhika. It was in Bali Nagar that Arun and Shobha had wonderful memories of family and friends. It was like a nice big carnival of our family members.

Rita Berry married Surinder Revri in 1969 in the Model Town House in Delhi, where our father, Late

Shri Ram Parshad Berry, and his third wife (or our third mother Uma Berry) and their two sons Sunil Berry and Vikram Berry lived. Our father left all his wealth to both Sunil and Vikram Berry.

Life without one's wife is not the best in the world—God wanted man and woman to live together because that is the way nature intended. When human beings lived during the Stone Age, this concept was not there; however, with the progress made in civilization over thousands of years, people worldwide—especially in India—realized how important it was. It was then that the act of marriage was created, with the lady choosing to marry a man, leave her home, live with her husband and take on the responsibilities of her husband's family.

Today we may call it by different names as denoted in the dictionary, but there is no doubt that this is one of the best ways God wanted us to live, and I think we have accepted it as we have progressed much more.

In our civilization. As we move into the 21st and 22nd centuries, it will be difficult to keep up with the changed definitions of marriage as people redefine it—like 'engaged' marriage—but still, one can clearly say that life without a wife is nothing.

I was thinking of this because, during the time I spent with Connie, I never thought that my life would change and that after her death, my life would become isolated. Arun is experiencing the same thing after losing Shobha.

I must say that with Shobha, Arun had good luck, as she was the queen of the household, handling everything and bringing fortune to him.

The moment our wives came into our lives, we felt happy and the blessings of God. Our wives were our soulmates, helped us inculcate our family values of humanity, and gave us the chance to make us feel welcome in society.

Pappi (Kiran) was the night and day of our lives, and another gift to our family was that our sister was married to a happy and positive person, Surinder Revri. Both Connie and Shobha were fond of each other and enjoyed the company of our wonderful family members, children, and granddaughters in Delhi. Their daughter was also very fond of Connie.

Both of us brothers miss our soulmates very much, and our brother-in-law Surinder no doubt misses our sister (his late wife), Kiran. What is the answer to this? Just suffering, or can we overcome the shock of missing our wives? We must remember and admit that we were very close to them indeed, who was in turn loved by our family members in Delhi, India, and Evanston, USA.

Shobha, Connie, and Kiran were very big-hearted women—they believed in humanity and kept good relationships with others in society. This wonderful gift has been studied at Harvard University, the USA, which says that no matter what profession you are in—from doctors and chartered accountants to scientists—the common thing to be happy is to maintain good relationships with others.

The three great women in our lives are in our thoughts and prayers as we move forward and help others in need. We have more empathy and understanding of love, thoughts, relationships, faults, and repentance through them. At this moment, we have lots of regrets about our lives and our understandings and misunderstandings. But we have to live with them and think of ourselves as high school or college students and improve ourselves—no matter what we have to do—to make up for our mistakes and faults.

It is a pity that so many errors were made by us unintentionally, purely out of ignorance. Will our regrets haunt us like ghosts? What about certain actions—will they, too, haunt us forever? Now, when we realize the painful regrets, we ask forgiveness from our wives and God. A learned man once told Pradeep that God would never forgive that person unless one asks for forgiveness from the person one hurts. It makes sense. Never do anything you have to regret in your life. Think before you act and speak only when asked to speak. Listening is silver, and silence is golden, whereas only a fool keeps talking.

Shobha and Connie kept silent and didn't argue. They had lots of patience could control their anger amazingly well.

Both Shobha and Connie were great cooks—fond of cooking different dishes that family and friends relished. Hospitality was in their blood, mirrored by our dear sister Pappi (Kiran), who was very hospitable like a queen.

Shobha, Connie, and Kiran adjusted with their husbands—they embodied tolerance, adjustment, caring, love, trust, and faith. With great passion and humanity, they adjusted to the circumstances of life with their husbands selflessly.

Who can return these jewels to us? We are silent on this great topic, as we don't know the answer, and even if we do know the answer, we're all lost in the pain of losing our loved ones. None of us ever had an argument with our wives—not over money or over an inheritance.

When families have too much wealth, money becomes a disease that fights for a bigger piece of the pie by maximizing one's inheritance—no matter if you lose your happiness and peace of mind. Isn't that sick?

It's wrong and unethical for the whole family to suffer over who gets what inheritance, to the extent that one battles depression while running to the court dealing with legal cases all your life. Keep away from all this, and enjoy the wonderful gift of the family while you can. The darkness of greed can cause great suffering in life.

Thanks to the Lord, we were both very lucky to have wonderful wives.

Kiran, our sister, was someone special to us—her love was like an ocean, just like Connie's. Shobha was a housewife as per Indian culture. At the same time, Connie was a wonderful housewife and an earning professor of Spanish, German, and French who could be self-sufficient in her income. This was when Indian society didn't make an effort to allow most women to work outside the house.

Arun and Shobha lived in a beautiful bungalow that had everything they needed. Both Shobha and Connie could help Arun since Shobha's father was always available to help the couple with financial help. The same was true for Connie's support of Pradeep.

This situation was due to our father's lack, whose third wife practically wanted to give all the family inheritance to her two biological sons. This caused some tension within the family and strained our resources, and we had to live on what we had.

Frankly, Shobha married Arun when they were financially decently well-off—and as time progressed, Arun started getting promotions with increasingly higher incomes. Pradeep married Connie, who later helped him study for an MBA at the Kellogg Graduate School of Management at Northwestern University, Evanston, Illinois, USA. Kiran, being a homemaker, was looked after well too, despite no help from our father, whose money perhaps was abused by his own wife's brother. We have no grudges against our father and stepmother, and we pray for their blessings.

It was part of our destiny to have these wonderful women in our lives. They left no bad memories or grudges, for which we're all very grateful to them.

December 20, 2019, was a day of great shock for us when Kiran unexpectedly died. I was in Delhi at that time.

I am writing a book about this, mentioning Pappi and Rita Berry. Lali and Pappi saw the death of the second mother at Dr. HC Trehan's, an ENT specialist across the Plaza Cinema, on November 17, 1951. Pappi was one hour old when our second mother died. For her last rites, her body was kept at 97 Thomson Road, Near Minto or Odeon Cinema, New Delhi. Our father married outside the family for his third marriage, and this was to Rita Berry. She produced her biological sons, Sunil and Vikram Berry. While Arun and I were raised by our grandparents, Sunil and Vikram were given all the privileges of the family. But we give thanks to our grandparents for giving Arun and me a great education, which was our assets to build successful careers—especially for Pradeep, who left for the US in 1976.

It was there that I met Constance Ann Fuller, Ph.D., which resulted in love at first sight and later a happy marriage for four decades.

References:

My Connie on Amazon and Google
www.bookofmyconnie.com
www.myconnie.com
www.pradeepberry.com
www.myconnie.net
Pradeep Berry on Google and YouTube

Our heart is at ease knowing that what was meant for us will never miss us and that what misses us was never meant for us. So, in either case, we need to have patience and have a strong belief that everything is happening for our good.

However, can we do that? We must be honest and say, write, talk, or cry, and admit, no? No!

No, we're not getting to accept and can bear it temporarily. We must have been very unhappy with these people who raised this issue; we started ignoring them forever, as it is our loss and not theirs! Ours was ours forever, but others thought for not ever?

The word and world want us to believe that it was destiny and we have no control over what we lost, but we were not convinced. We will keep remembering them, who were ours and ours forever, and that is fine for us.

Our happiness and unhappiness, both as our happiness, are in both ways. We would miss what we lost.

Arun Berry is a graduate of one of the top colleges in Delhi, the University of Delhi, and a postgraduate from the Law College in Delhi. He is a retired pharmaceutical officer, a learned classical singer, and a composer who has performed various classical music concerts in metropolitan areas of Delhi. He is the father of two boys and has a daughter-in-law and two granddaughters.

His younger biological brother Pradeep Berry is a retired banker and an author of six books written for his wife, Connie Berry. They all live together in a joint family, which Arun Berry and his wonderful family have maintained in Delhi. He has been very kind to extend his help for this book, dedicated to his sister-in-law or bhabhi, Shobha.

Thanks to our wonderful readers for acknowledging this book of our love for Shobha.

If only we had wisdom when we were young and brought up without the need for greed and cheating our own family, this world would be a much better place than the one right now.

I believe the source of the most misery is greed and sloth. Countries whose people are accustomed to hard work embody the meaning of happiness in life—such as Japan, Norway, the US, and Iceland. From them, we can learn to try and persist in attaining happiness in our own lives and attaining our dreams.

Let's not forget the Lord, for prayers have a very soothing effect on the troubled mind, making dreams come true. Miracles happen every day, so don't deprive people of that hope, for that may be the only thing they may have.

Shobha, Kiran, and Connie proved that happiness and obstacles are part of the ups and downs of our lives in our lives. Thanks for your wonderful gifts and blessings, Shobha Berry, wife of my elder brother, Arun Berry. Thanks to Connie, my late wonderful wife. Thanks to our late sister Pappi, whose demise was our most recent loss.

Our thoughts would be in our lives throughout our lives, and in our family, 'til Shobha, Connie and Kiran come back in our lives and keep reincarnating many more times.

Shobha was a great fan of TV, Facebook, iPad, watching Indian movies, episodes, TV series, and listening to old songs and different programs—especially when she was suffering from vascular problems and had lots of pain throughout day and night.

Before her vascular problems, Shobha was a party woman with her husband, Arun. He was married to Marjorie Hopkins or Marjorie Behl. Shobha was very much interested in traveling with her husband Arun and her family. She often traveled to London, Liverpool, and America to visit Pradeep and our cousin Vanita Sarin, whose father was a great dermatologist in India and abroad.

There are many different memories in our lives to share with our readers worldwide, but books can't be burdened with each instance of life.

As stated before, Arun and Shobha lived in Katra Neel from 1978 to July 2000 and then moved to Rohini, where Arun currently stays with his two sons, Ashiem and Ashish, his daughter-in-law Mona; and granddaughters Krishna and Radhika.

Pradeep goes to visit practically every year—including seven times with his wife, Connie. Her last trip was from February 9, 2004, to March first, 2004. Although she would have liked to go, circumstances were different, and she was very happy to see. I can visit every year, and I would have loved her to come with me as I was very miserable without my Connie darling.

Shobha was a noble, innocent wife, and so were Connie and Kiran (our wonderful sister). Thanks to our good karmas, we have our wonderful wives.

Pradeep still has a great consulting firm for crisis management, mergers, commercial lending, leverage funding, syndication, cash flow, bankruptcy act, investment banking with an evaluation of collateral and personal guarantee or junk bonds.

However, he stopped working after his wife was operated on in 2005 and spent all his time with Connie.

Connie treated her husband to first-class trips to Hawaii in 2006 and 2007 and Las Vegas, Norwegian Cruise, and paid for the ticket to visit his family in Delhi each year until her death.

Connie was paying all the expenses, food, and travel in the world until the fateful day of her death in 2015.

Connie and Pradeep took a wonderful trip from the University of Michigan in April 1998 to Italy, visiting Cortana, Tuscany, and Florence. They went on many other tours—to Norway in 2007; Ireland, Hungary, and the Netherlands in 2009 to Austria, where they visited Mozart's House. They also visited the Vienne Symphony, where they played Connie's wish for Laura's theme.

We must learn from a tiger or lion that they only capture their prey in the jungles when hungry. After that, they do not harm the animals unless hungry—whereas humans fight and kill for greed, no matter how much wealth they have. They are still hungry for more to get.

It's our happiness to write that both Shobha and Connie were tigers, born to be wonderful humanitarians. They were born to help others in trouble and suffering. It was a wonderful gift and a great peaceful joy to see the Lord in their brain, minds, body, heart, and souls, which we can't ever forget in our lives.

Therefore, we both decided to write our thoughts about our lives with our great wives.

Our wives were our assets for the future and the lives we were enjoying with them. Now, without them and after their demise, our lives and thoughts are different, and their thoughts are with us and in our heart and soul, where they would remain forever.

We must remember our wonderful wives, no matter what life takes us.

It is a message to our children—to teach them about humanity and happiness in serving the needy and fighting to remove poverty from the world. We can put our thoughts and foundations to our own family to help others in need, in memories of our wonderful wives and our lives with them.

Shobha always lived in Delhi, and she died in the third house she moved to, where she was with her husband Arun, sons Ashiem and Ashish, daughter-in-law Mona, and granddaughters Krishna and Radhika. Connie last visited on February 9, 2004—after that, she didn't visit.

Mona Gulati was not married to Ashish until April 15, 2005, Krishna was born, and Radhika. Pradeep, too stayed with them whenever he came to Delhi. Shobha, per Arun, brought him a great life of happiness, and the same with Pradeep too with his wife, who was the best part of his life.

For Arun, she was a saraniye (no words for her praise is in the dictionary), pujaniye (wife is worth worshipping), and vandinay (lives in my heart and soul with happiness).

There are a lot of great studies at Harvard University, USA, about the happiness of students, doctors, scientists, chartered accountants, medical representatives, and others in Delhi, India, and those all over the world. The results reflected a common understanding that people who had maintained a peaceful relationship with others are the happiest and love to be with humanity and live a peaceful life.

Connie was the best example of this, as well as our own Shobha and my sister Kiran. My late uncle Dr.PN Behl, his English wife Marjorie, and daughter Vanita were very kind to the poor and needy people. The same was true with Arun, his boys, daughters-in-law, and our granddaughters, who are a wonderful gift for getting involved in the lives of humanity and the happiness for others. What are our mornings, evenings, and nights coming around to in this global movement of humanity from darkness to darkness? Well, we have a wonderful gift to humanity, for our happiness is to serve the Lord and our karmas.

What goes around comes around in our lifetime only? I would like to see an innovation and marketing management for humanity to eliminate poverty from the earth, which is possible if we are determined by our sanskar or foundation as taught by our parents, family, and teachers.

Our story and values are drawn from our culture, instilled in us since we began to go to school in Delhi. Our wonderful grandparents taught us the values of life, which we used once we got married to keep our foundation strong. Those values and foundations became handy in our lives both in India and the USA.

The most important part of our relationship with our wives was that we all performed our part gracefully.

The both of us grew up together under our grandparents' care in Old Delhi, in the circumstances beyond their control and with lots of suffering and unhappiness after the death of their mother, their second mother too. Our father remarried a third time, and our stepmother separated the three of us children's father over issues of inheritance of wealth.

Thanks to our lovely wives, we are here today—two boys who didn't have a clue how to write a book. The loss of our wives—Connie in 2015 and Shobha in 2018—was very heavy on us.

Pradeep has written 14 books, as mentioned in his Who's Who profile.

Both Arun and Pradeep decided to write a book on Shobha in honor of her wonderful life. Arun lives in Delhi, while Pradeep lives in Evanston, USA. They both have been working on this book together.

> *"You are good when you strive to give of yourself. Yet you are not evil when you seek gain for yourself. For to the fruit, giving is a need, as receiving is a need to the root."*
>
> — Kahlil Gibran

Both of us have followed the teachings of Mahatma Gandhi, Kahlil Gibran, The Holy Gita, Ramayana, Bible, Quran, Lord Buddha, Tulsidas, Chankya, and Swami Vivekanananda. This helped us get a better perspective of ourselves, our lives, family values, and most importantly, our wonderful wives and family.

We often love to have arguments with God to return our wives, if it is possible. Yes, only God can grant our happiness back.

Shobha was the night and day of our family in India, whereas Connie was the same in the US. Connie and Pradeep used to visit Delhi quite often to visit our family members. Since they are in our thoughts, we pray for them and the wonderful times with our Shobha, Connie, and sister Kiran. We can talk about our wives for thousands of pages, but that is too much to ask from our readers.

Shobha was a kind, simple wife and was happy in all circumstances. She had no complaints, and Connie was the same way. Both of them were loved by their husbands and children. Carylon K Berry or Kiran Berry' a great morning daughter who could not get a wink of sleep without her mom Connie and father, Pradeep Berry. It was a wonderful time but, things keep on changing with life and time.

In this biography of Shobha, Arun and Pradeep put their hearts' passion to remember her and Pradeep's wife Connie, who died in 2015. Both are not physically with us, but spiritually, they make us believe they are watching over us. This is the best way to get over the grief and suffering. The detailed chapters describe our wonderful lives together in separate chapters of the book.

Our priority had always been to make the best of our lifelong marriage, with no separation or divorce allowed—nor did we ever talk or think about it. It is a part of our wonderful culture and ethical approach. Once you're married, it's a lifetime commitment. We don't go out to marry again—even if the unfortunate demise creates a loss, we wouldn't have a second marriage because of our love for our wives.

Shobha was a night owl—she used to watch TV, movies, and serials until early in the morning. That habit of hers gave Arun the leverage to stay up late with her, watching movies and drinking the coffee, tea, and sweets she made.

When Pradeep and Connie visited each year from the USA to see the family, Shobha was the home's life. A life of happiness and fun disappeared after her death and of Connie.

Arun and Pradeep feel honored to write a wonderful book about their wonderful wives. We both brothers decided to write down our wonderful thoughts to express our happiness and memories in this book. We must also remember our wonderful sister Rita Berry/Kiran Revri, who died in 2019.

Our family members have always lived in our ancestral house in Old Delhi, where Pradeep migrated to Chicago in 1976.

We must love our wonderful life partners every day of our life. Your wife is the best part of your lifetime. She wishes to see her husband succeed in his life and expects only love. We can do for them what they do for their family.

Shobha was a great fan of dresses, cosmetics, perfumes, and sarees—especially Indian style dresses, lipsticks of dark brown color, and purses of different sizes and colors. She was the light of our wonderful home during parties, and Connie, too, enjoyed the best clothing. Our family and friends loved both Shobha and Connie, and along with our sister Kiran would laugh over many things. Shobha was great at keeping family issues within the family, and no gossip was warranted with her.

Both Shobha and Connie made our souls happy—now we realize our loss.

Kiran's husband, Surinder Revri, was a good husband and brother-in-law, whose help was instrumental in Pradeep going to the US in 1976.

Thanks to all three—Connie, Shobha, and Kiran for giving us those wonderful memories of life and teaching us not to waste time fighting. Kiran (Pappi) was the soul of our second mother—'Kanta mummy.'

Shobha was also very fond of cutlery, kitchen appliances, cell phones, tablets. She was a fan of TV shows—especially Indian serials. TV was the most important part of her life, but she was happy, especially when talking with Arun and their sons Ashiem and Ashish. Pradeep would be very happy to be with Shobha, talking late into the night in Arun's living room. Both of them would talk about life in the US, about Connie, her parents, brothers, and about Carylon Berry and her school and college.

Shobha was very fond of girl children, and she was very keen to adopt a girl, but it was very difficult. Shobha was very quiet about this and kept it to herself. We respected her for being an honest person.

When Connie and Pradeep visited Delhi, Shobha would talk about life in Delhi and would ask how different it was in the US from the heat, sun, fan, air conditioner, movies, and travel in India.

There are so many great peaceful memories of Shobha and Connie, which are wonderful to talk about and write about—but too much writing will be difficult for our readers.

Our lives and happiness were linked with our family values and our wonderful ancestors. Now we have lost a whole lot of family members, and we feel somewhat lonely. This is mitigated by our coming generations—Krishna, Radhika, and Carylon Berry.

We must have our prayers for Shobha this year on November 8, 2020, when it would be two years since Shobha has gone like the wind.

In our lifetime, we're all confused about our future spouses—should we marry or not, from inside the family or outside the family, love marriage, engagement by our family members and grandparents who are our wonderful well-wishers— but marriages are wonderful God's blessings to our family and friends. We must love, care and support our wives. She would be a great asset in our old age, besides our younger and middle ages and could be vice versa. Based upon the true stories, this saying is more relevant, and the younger readers would be happy to learn the life when they reach advanced age. Don't forget them and remember the suggestions given in this book.

Can we get the same? Our fate. Thanks for our wonderful fate to have Shobha Berry. Our happy thoughts are with you.

Adorable and unforgettable Shobha. Life?

That is why people should think of writing, if not full, but a small biography or even some highlights of their life. At the same time, people with spiritual knowledge would not fear death, knowing that we all have to go and that it's a part of life. If they had a good and healthy life, they would know that *sadda naam to parmatama ka hai*.

Marne ke baad or paidai hone sey pehle hamara koi kissi sey rishta nahi hai, but sometimes it is different from adopting that attitude. Before his death, or even long before, he only desired that his five institutions, whom he always called his Temples, be looked after for humanity, and that what he was requesting from me and other doctors and trustees. Each person behaves differently, and some say their purpose of life has been accomplished, and they face no threat of death.

It's that power to write our own life and happiness in our lives for humanity, and our coming generations, to know who we are and how we were raised in our lives. Who were they, and what were all our thoughts about ourselves and our family values and values of humanity? Only, we're going to be able to make a gift of remembering our ancestors and our family life and our history of what and where we came, we have to teach our value system in our lives for future and prolonged lives we have shared partly due to their own lives and education including school, college, and post-graduation.

Keep your thoughts and prayers for others too.

It's a wonderful game for the coming generations of the future.

Both Arun and Pradeep Berry started writing this wonderful book in May 2020. Things happen at the proper time of their own, and it's an unexpected gift for humanity to help us in our unhappiness of life to bring happiness again in some way or the other. Miracles happen every day, so don't deprive someone of hope. Hope may be the only thing they may have. It's with that hope we, both the brothers, discussed our thoughts in this wonderful book.

As such, this book is dedicated to our wonderful gift of God Shobha Berry and Constance Ann Berry. Shobha and Connie were two special daughters-in-law. Shobha was the first daughter-in-law, and Connie was the second daughter-in-law of our wonderful family in India and the USA. Both Shobha and Connie were very close, were raised in the most wonderful family environments, and had characters with ethics and hospitality. That is the best way to define their love towards the husbands and family values with other great qualities.

We are in the hands of our Lord, the wonderful Supreme Court of the world, watching over us for good and bad deeds, our karmas. We must remember our family values and our wonderful gift of God to humanity, and happiness in our lives and others too, no matter what. But, we must do our duty in life. Life is a duty, and it should be performed in the best way for humanity and your family and friends. Once we do something good for others, we get some happiness, and before we do that, we should take care of our own family, children, grandchildren, or granddaughters who are in your family as a special gift of God and happiness. It is a very important part of our life to teach that daughters are God's wonderful gift to our family and not always the boys. Girls play a great role in our lives, sometimes much more than boys. My wife Connie told me right away after our marriage that daughters were responsible for looking after their parents in the US. I was surprised, as, in India, it was the boys or the eldest son.

Keep that in mind and think of a smart but pretty big face of humanity and humanitarian values in our lives for our next life and happiness for humanity, our family and friends, and our relationship with our wonderful family members. We must thank our Lord for our wonderful gift of God to bless us with happiness from our wife.

The book is our wonderful way to get over our sadness in losing our wonderful wife's Shobha and Connie, Pappi was our wonderful sister who brought us happiness, but she died in India on December 20, 2019. It was so sad to see her dead. It brought a lot of sadness in our lives and felt so bad for our family and friends, especially for Pappi's husband Surinder Revri, son Rajesh, daughter-in-law Pooja and grandson Bonny; Pappi's daughter

Priya, son-in-law Raju, granddaughter Krishkaand, and grandson Mannu. We must remember the most important part of our life to maintain the relationship with our Pappi's family. Her mother sacrificed her life for Arun and Pradeep.

Thanks to our readers for choosing our book to be a great gift of God and happiness for humanity and happiness in our lives. This book enlightens many people—lifetime values of our childhood and adulthood lives.

Some of our wonderful gifts for the coming generations and newlyweds, to see the old tradition of our culture in the future. As far as Shobha and Connie were concerned, they both applied the culture very well. Shobha used to work for hours and hours to cook the food for her family, including our family and friends. She was a wonderful cook, and it kept her busy. Many people have left us for heaven, and new generations are busy, and we don't have a charm for cooking food, except the maid lady or Mona Berry.

We are unhappy that our wonderful wives are no longer with us, and we all miss them to the same extent as a fish without water. It gets very difficult to find ourselves in the way we used to be. Thanks to our wonderful wives for giving us a great peaceful life.

The gap of our wife's death was our loss and suffering. However, our thoughts are with you all the time. Shobha,

the pillar of the Berry family, was a wonderful gift to Arun, whose day and night remains still very unhappy. But, it is mitigated by his sons, daughter-in-law, and granddaughters Krishana and Radhika, who have their charm.

> *Everything on earth lives according to the law of nature, and from that law emerges the glory and joy of liberty, but man is denied this fortune because he set a limited and earthly law of his own for the God-given soul. Man built a narrow and painful prison in which he secluded his affections and desires.*
>
> — Kahlil Gibran

Who is responsible for the demise of our wives? God or medical doctors? Who is powerful enough to give our lives happily with our wives? We must admit, it is God whose blessings can return our wives. Medical care was the best part of our wonderful wives, but God decided to take away our divine message.

> *A sincere man feels for the troubles and tribulations of others and tries his level best to alleviate their sufferings. He is very sympathetic, soft-hearted, and also generous. He is always*

reliable, quite frank, honest, and true. He is free from crookedness, hypocrisy, cheating, and double-dealing. People place implicit faith in his words.

— Swami Shardanand

Authors' Viewpoint on Life and Happiness

WE MUST LOVE, care and support our wives. She would be a great asset in our old age, besides a companion in our younger and middle ages. Based upon true stories, this saying is more relevant, and younger readers can benefit from the suggestions given in this book.

This wonderful book is a tribute to our wives, Shobha and Connie.

We are in the hands of our Lord, who is watching over our good and bad deeds and our karmas.

Keep in mind humanitarian values, which will help us in our lives and our next.

Our Wives

Our wives are a wonderful gift for a lifetime, especially as we age.

For a wife, the loss of her husband is a great shock—especially in her older days. This sacred relationship between a husband and wife is sacred and to be cherished, no matter what life has to offer.

Adorable and Unforgettable Wife, Shobha

The both of us—Arun and Pradeep Berry—take pride in writing our tributes to our wonderful wives, Shobha and Connie Berry. They were two wonderful gifts from God and blessings to our families. We have decided not to dwell on the past and instead think of our life partners' happiness.

Shobha Berry was educated in Nainital, a hill station built by the British as a resort for the summer holidays. Constance Ann Berry was an American. Both brothers are lucky to have had wonderful wives for 46 and 43 years, respectively. At the same time, we brothers give our tributes and prayers to our late sister Kiran Revri

(originally Rita Berry, who married Surinder Revri), who we loved dearly but lost in 2019.

Arun, Pradeep, and Surinder are now widowers but are lucky to have had such wonderful life partners.

One of the most important themes of our culture has been the wonderful, sincere, and pure, sacred relationship between husband and wife. Connie used to tell Pradeep that a wife and her husband should be best friends, besides being a couple. This is why it's very upsetting when one has passed away—only then do we realize the importance.

It is so sad to see many people losing their spouses and suffering from a mountain of depression and suffering throughout their lives. Only then does the realization of love come, as it becomes very difficult to be alone—regardless of whether one has children and grandchildren. Your second half is missing, and one feels alone in the night, and prayers become our power. Music and songs, especially devotional songs, have a soothing effect on troubled minds and souls.

Shobha taught us in the early years not to be carried away into the darkness by freeloaders. Connie told Pradeep the same thing in the USA. Both of them were against the rich freeloaders for scotch, sodas, and liquor. Shobha adjusted in all circumstances of happiness and unhappiness.

Love is a double-edged sword—you know what love is, but it is very painful to love someone and lose that person. However, if you didn't love someone, you would not know what love is.

Love is a wonderful duty we carry throughout our lifetime—to our wives, to parents, to grandparents, to grandchildren and friends—unless one becomes a saint and moves to the Himalaya mountains, or the jungles and lives with the animals while sleeping on the grass and eating fruits and vegetables uncooked. If that happens, love of animals has a life of its own. Tarzan was a wonderful example if it's true.

Going back to our Shobha, whose unconditional love was a gift of God. Shobha was born with the gift of happiness and contentment. She was content—whether in our family home in Katra Neel, Bali Nagar, or when we finally moved to a different house.

She was happy wherever she lived with no complaints. She was a very strong woman determined to be a great wife, mother, grandparent, and sister-in-law. She was a great mother and mother-in-law to her young ones, whom she loved very much. She was born with love, passion, and happiness for others in her blood.

She wanted to live happily and wanted her family to live, but the cruel hands of God took her unexpectedly in 2018. What was the reason for her sudden death? It is a puzzling story and a very painful one for her family, especially for her husband and her brother-in-law Pradeep, who lost his American wife, Connie, in 2015.

Shobha was the best part of life for her husband, and she was close to Pradeep and Connie. We all loved Shobha.

Thanks, Shobha, for your kindness, thoughts, and contribution to our happiness and life with your smiles and blessings. Thanks for your thoughts on our wonderful lives. We all miss you, your presence, and your happiness. The house looks different and feels lonely without you.

Death of a Shuagan
Shobha Berry

BEFORE WE GIVE our tributes to our Shobha, we must say that it is an auspicious sign that a wife passes away in her husband's hands, not as a widow. Shobha died in Delhi on November 8, 2018. Pradeep's wife Connie's death also died in his hands in 2015 in Evanston, USA. We are both thankful to our Lord for this auspicious gift.

Constance Ann Berry, Ph.D., was Pradeep's soulmate. The only difference between her and Shobha was that Connie was an American who was born, raised, educated, married, and died in the USA. However, they both were very close to each other and were very happy to see each other in Delhi and the USA whenever we visited each other.

God took both of them, and only their husbands were alive. We both miss them due to our close relationship.

Connie was a wonderful wife, but her biological brother Mike Fuller and his wife's strong influence on him eventually strained their relationship. He was like a puppet in his wife's hands, manipulated into things.

However, we would like to write about the story of humanity and happiness in our life—a life which we lived with care and passion and the wonderful life of our karmas in this and future lives.

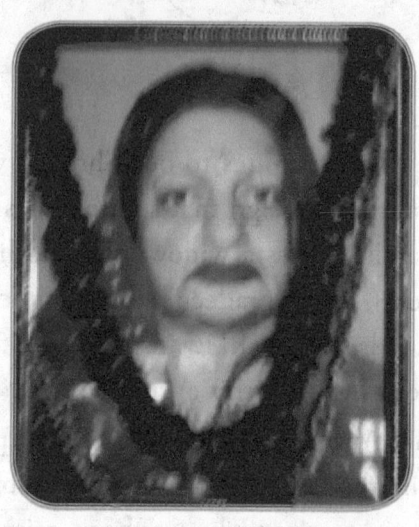

Preface and Authors' Note

ARUN AND PRADEEP, both of us want to thank our family—who we believe are God's greatest gifts.

Mothers are the greatest gift of God, although we lost ours when we were very young. Shanti mummy died when Arun was 11 months old, and Pradeep was two months old. Her younger sister Kanta married our father for happiness and died in childbirth while giving birth to our sister.

Our third mother ignored the three of us, who our father married from outside the family. The suffering of Arun, Pradeep, and sister Rita was great. We were brought up by our grandparents, who gave us everything we wanted.

It is to be noted that some people go through loss by crying over the death, others by drinking or smoking, or even by some humanitarian aid to help others and get peace of mind. People cope with depression and unhappiness after a setback, each in their way. In our case, our extreme loss was of our wives and sister—Shobha, Connie, and Rita/Kiran.

It all happened suddenly—three women in our lives left us, leaving us in difficult times.

Happiness and unhappiness come in pairs—today, they are synonymous with depression and anxiety, which is currently a terminology used in medical science. How come it was not used 300 or 500 years ago? In the family's hands, were there doctors prescribing anti-depression drugs like Zenox, Alprazolam, Clondin, Atenolol Lisinpro, Tylenol, and other drugs? Did we know about these? It was a wonderful invention for our brain and soul to cope with our thoughts and the stress we face in our lives. But, there is no other choice for the human body now, as our medical science has made us that way.

Our Childhood

OUR SANSKAR—OUR FOUNDATION, which we receive from childhood, instilled by parents and grandparents in conjunction with our teachers, became the most important part of our lives. It is a wonderful game that runs through all of our lives and others—to play with our duties and rights—but do we understand the difference between the two?

From childhood, we are in the hands of our parents and grandparents, who create the foundation of our lives by instilling education, character, ethics, honesty, selfless work, self-dependence, and the awareness of unhappiness and death. Also, we are taught to believe in karma, which is what we receive upon our death.

Therefore, we must remember our death and avoid doing anything bad to improve our karma, lead a good life, and honestly understand our circumstances. We must be happy in any circumstances, for God wants us to live and trust the power of our Lord, and do our best and leave the rest to Him.

Our teachers are our well-wishers in our life until we are in this world. We are what we learn and what we do with our lives. We are responsible for our destiny, as no one can make it except ourselves.

We must be happy in all the circumstances we live in, as we have no choice except to work hard and smart, and more importantly, to have human values. We are what we're taught.

We must remember the Lord in both the good and bad times of our lives. God is in our thoughts, prayers, body, and breathing and always wishes to soothe us. It takes a lot to come out from the shock and sickness of hurdles in our lives.

Your thoughts on the Lord and prayers addressed to Him have a very soothing effect on the troubled mind. We must remember to thank the Lord before going to bed and when we wake up in the morning, for our bodies are a wonderful gift from the Almighty, which allows us to preserve humanity, our family, and our children. We must have control over our character and carnal desires, which can ruin our lives, happiness, and moral values with no compromise.

Philosophy of Happiness and Life Partners in our Lifetime

Are we born alone, and do we die alone? Perhaps we all know the answer to that. Still, a wonderful gift from God is to be reminded again and again of our happiness and duty, especially towards our coming generations. Thanks to our wonderful ancestors who lived wonderful lifetimes, we learned a lot from them during our childhood. It affected how we lived as husbands, wives, children, grandparents and grandchildren, and many more roles. No one has taken a dime with them at the time of their demise, proving that we all were born empty-handed and died empty-handed. Having said that, we must follow the Lord during both the times of happiness and unhappiness—both sisters in everybody's life.

PERENNIAL LOVE

Biological Brothers

BOTH OF US, brothers Arun and Pradeep Berry, are no more than the power of the god. Realization comes from the experience and lifetime values of humanity and happiness and sacrifices to our wonderful life and soul to learn from our own experiences of life.

We both were very lucky to have had excellent wives—Arun's wife Shobha was Indian while Pradeep's wife Connie was an American born in Glenview, Illinois, USA. Sadly, both of them were taken away by the cruel hands of the Lord.

Constance 'Connie' Ann Berry, Ph.D., a professor of Spanish, German and French, died on February 27, 2015, in Evanston Hospital in Evanston, Illinois, USA. Arun's wife Shobha died on November 8, 2018, in New Delhi, India.

A third loss was of our half-sister, who died on December 20, 2019, in Gurgaon, India. These three personal losses very shook us. Our sister's mother (our stepmother) had died in childbirth, and all three of us were raised by our grandparents (mother's parents), who was born to help our childhood. Our father married three times, each due to the death of his previous spouse. From the third marriage, we have two half-brothers who are the beneficiaries of our father's inheritances, and not us three—Arun, Pradeep, and sister Rita Berry or Pappi. Such is life, though, and one must have the wonderful gift of passion and happiness to go through it happily.

The Life of the Authors

OUR OWN LIVES have been full of challenges and happiness, as is the norm for all true-life stories—this is true for all unless they are fictional characters in stories. However, Pradeep is a believer in true stories based upon life values. Most authors are great for the values and education in writing books, but others aren't recognized until they leave this earth. Many wonderful authors have not gotten recognition until they have gone from our lives, and it is only later that our society recognizes them. Thanks for their wonderful contributions in this world of good and bad.

We are doing a great sin to ourselves by our greed through a selfish act against God. No one can find out the reasoning behind this game for future generations. Only

God knows what the best way to make a better system of happiness and life is.

Humanity is the most wonderful gift of God—the Lord's blessings for our wonderful soul. We are no writers or authors, but we get our happiness and unhappiness with the Lord through God's blessings and prayers for our healing therapy.

Tributes to Shobha Berry

BOTH BROTHERS DECIDED to write a book for our wonderful Shobha, wife of Arun and sister-in-law of Pradeep. Shobha was the mother of two sons, Ashiem and Ashish; mother-in-law of Mona Berry; and grandmother of Krishna and Radhika. Her husband called 'Kashmiri Apple'—a sign of happiness, love, and care.

The marriage between Arun and Shobha was the epitome of a lifetime of happiness for our family. After her death, Arun misses her a lot, but perhaps she is better off by not suffering from the pain she had undergone from vascular veins, which left her sinking with weakness and made it difficult to eat. In the end, Shobha was mostly bedridden and had to be looked after 24x7 by nurses in her house.

In addition to Arun, the rest of the extended family gave great moral support to Shobha. As he called her, Pradeep especially doted on his bhabhi (elder brother's wife)—a wonderful term from Indian culture. A bhabhi is like a mother in our culture because from the beginning of our childhood. We're always taught to respect our elders. Hospitality has a special place in our way of life, and to take care of our guests, friends, neighbors and pay respect to elders are the base values of our culture

Shobha died in Delhi, India, on November 8, 2018. Her death came three years after Pradeep's wife Connie died in Evanston, the USA, in 2015, which left him heartbroken. We thank the Lord for the wonderful gifts of our wives.

Our Wonderful Family

THERE ARE MANY more important people in our lives who we wish to mention and send wishes to. We give our tributes to Shobha's parents—father KL Khanna and mother Santosh Khanna—who were a very great part of both our lives. Mr. Khanna was the first person to visit Connie and Pradeep in Evanston after their marriage in July 1979, and he stayed for three weeks.

We also wish to give tributes to our uncle Dr. PN Behl, his English wife Marjorie, and daughter Vanita, who also visited the US in September 1979. Now they are no more in this world but are in our hearts.

Shobha and Connie were the life of our family. New Delhi was the family's headquarters for the most part—especially Bali Nagar, at the house of Arun and Shobha. Our late maternal grandfather, Shri ID Mehra, was the most important part of our lives ever since our brothers were born. Our childhood was possible because of his children—our five aunts and two uncles—who helped raise us and our sister Rita or Pappi (our half-sister from our second mother Kanta or 'Kanta mummy').

Rita, too died on December 20, 2019. It was a great shock and loss to us, especially to our brothers and her son, daughter, in-laws, grandchildren, and husband, Surinder Revri. Her death reminded us of how our family on our mother's side were the great sufferers who had raised her and both of us after the death of Kanta mummy, our wonderful second mother.

Shobha Berry – A Wonderful Wife

Shobha, we must confess, was an adorable, unforgettable, beautiful soul who became Arun's best friend and brought great luck into his life. She was a great star of Arun's extended family and relations in India. Our late uncle, Dr. PN Behl, and his English wife and children were very close to all of us. We were a very happy family—close to each other, and Shobha and Pradeep's wife Connie, too, shared a close relationship even though Connie lived in the USA.

Pradeep used to come to visit us quite often at Connie's insistence, as she was adamant that Pradeep should visit his family, especially since her family was already in the USA. Thanks to Connie for her sacrifices—she stayed with her books and busied herself writing theses while Pradeep visited Delhi to see his family.

Shobha and Arun were married for 46 years. She fondly and lovingly called him Berry sahib. Shobha never tolerated anything against her loving husband, no matter what. She learned Facebook like a computer wizard and often spent a lot of time on that. Otherwise, she would spend time watching TV serials and movies.

Shobha and Arun would sit in the living room and talk about their family and friends' lives and often sing the Gurvani—Sikh religious songs or bhajans. She would always bring gifts and presents for family and friends. It was in her blood to make friends all over the world through Facebook and keep in touch with family friends.

Further, she brought Arun luck in every aspect, from the moment she entered our ancestral house in Katra Neel in 1972 to the time of her demise in 2018 at our third home in Rohini. After so many great memories and some unhappy episodes—which are always part of our lives—it was eventually time for his luck to run its course.

Pradeep's Wife, Connie

PRADEEP LEFT FOR the US on January 15, 1976, and met Constance 'Connie' Ann Fuller merely days later. It was love at first sight, which led to a court marriage on January 28, 1976. They spent a wonderful marriage together spanning four decades, during which time she endeared herself to everyone, including Arun and Shobha. It is worth mentioning that Connie was a star in the US and also in India with her husband's family. She was a wonderful soul and beloved by all.

Harrowing Childhood Memoirs

Pradeep's pain after Connie's death in 2015 and Arun's shock at Shobha's demise in 2018 was a very difficult time for both of us. Our childhood had been tough since our biological mother died when Arun and Pradeep were only 11 months and two months of age, respectively. The bond between us was the most important part of our relationship as we were two brothers with no mother—this stayed even after our father married a second time, from which we had a very dear half-sister in 1951.

The struggle, depression, lack of happiness, and money were the most difficult things in our lives then. We are thankful to God for blessing us with our grandparents, who looked after us even as our third mom (stepmother) didn't even care about the both of us and our younger sister. Our stepmother wanted her happiness by having her children with our father. Once our biological mother died, our father became a father only for the sake of it—whether out of fear of his third wife or not?

This was very difficult for the three of us—Arun, Pradeep, and sister Rita. Both Arun and Pradeep are widowed, and our sister has also left us and her husband Surinder.

What is the answer? Thanks for your thoughts.

Marriage is Wonderful

Marriage was the most important part of our lives, and we loved our wives dearly. We learned this wonderful character from our grandparents, who had a wonderful time giving us the best possible life and making us feel loved in our family—as part of everyone's life.

Beginning of our Love
– Arun and Shobha

It was February 15, 1972, in Bengalimarket, New Delhi, when Arun's parents decided to arrange his marriage to a beautiful girl, Shobha Khanna, who was from Delhi itself. The sun was shining that day, and it was very pleasant to sit in the family garden.

KL Khanna and his wife had approached Arun's family to see if he would be interested in marrying their daughter, as is the custom in traditional Indian culture. Arun saw Shobha and immediately said yes—it was love at first sight for the both of them. Arun recalls that it was the best decision he ever made—he felt as if he had known her for a thousand years. Shobha also felt the same. Both of them liked each other and were excited to get married. Their marriage lasted 46 years from 1972 onwards until Shobha died on November 8, 2018, leaving Arun heartbroken and alone to suffer silently. She is survived by sons Ashiem and Ashish, daughter-in-law Mona and two granddaughters, Krishana and Radhika.

Another Player in our Lives

O<small>N</small> F<small>EBRUARY</small> 28, 2015, her death at 1:10 a.m. in Evanston hospital was crushing news for all of us. The younger brother, Pradeep, is suffering from the unexpected loss of his American-born wife, Connie. Apart from Pradeep's grief, it was difficult for Arun and Shobha, who were very close to Connie.

Thanks to Shobha and Connie for being strong women partners and wonderful souls. They were soulmates to the two brothers, Arun and Pradeep, born of Shanti Berry, who died when they were 11 months and two months old, respectively.

Our father married her younger sister, 'Kanta Mummy,' as his second wife, and after five years and four months, our sister Rita Berry was born. But Kanta mummy died after giving birth to Rita, starting a very difficult time of our lives from November 1951.

Childhood Life

OUR FATHER MARRIED a woman from outside the family for the third time, and her presence caused big problems since she wanted to have her children with our father. What choice did our father have? And what choices did we have but to suffer her thoughts and actions?

The rejection of us three from her life resulted in suffering for all of us, including our father and grandparents on both sides. Action brings reactions, and reaction brings actions, which result in childhood of suffering.

Shobha also had to accept that suffering, but her being lucky for Arun, things were beginning to look better and better than at Katra Neel. Shobha's father, late Shri KL Khanna, was determined to get the couple a wonderful place in Bali Nagar, New Delhi—a wonderful stroke of good fortune and happiness for the family. At the same time, Pradeep left for the US, where he met and married Connie in Chicago, which led to a life of wonderful success.

Shobha's Children

Shobha bore two sons—Ashiem and Ashish Berry. Pradeep Berry left for the USA in 1976 but kept coming to Delhi occasionally and traveled in India and the world. Perhaps it was the best part of Pradeep's life, which was turned upside down by Connie's death on February 27, 2015.

On November 8, 2018, Shobha's death was too shocking on our sister Rita Berry, who died on December 20, 2019.

Shobha was the Ultimate

GOING BACK TO Shobha, she was born in her happiness and lived life according to her choices. Her father's support was a wonderful gift from time to time for both Shobha and naturally to Arun too, who was just starting his career with a great pharmaceutical company in Delhi.

Shobha's entrance into Arun's life brought more happiness and prosperity than ever. This included a car, a scooter, and a house in a very nice and expensive suburb of Delhi. All their relationships with family members were strong. Pradeep got married in the US to the wonderful Connie, who became a source of happiness in our lives.

Both Connie and Shobha were very happy to be with each other and were good friends besides close relations.

Shobha in USA and England

SHOBHA WENT TO Liverpool and London to see her brother along with our cousin, Vanita Sarin. From there, they proceeded to spend time with Pradeep and Connie in Evanston, USA and had a wonderful time with them.

Shobha and Vanita visited several places—Great America in Gurnee Illinois; Lake Geneva in Wisconsin; the Baha'i Temple in Evanston; and also the wonderful Indian market Devon Avenue, which was full of life with Indian food, restaurants, clothing, fabrics, sarees, and ladies clothing which were not available during that time in India. The both of them had a wonderful time together.

Shobha extended her trip by two weeks and also missed her flight because of overweight luggage. British Airways was nice enough to help her fly the very next day. It was her first international trip, but Shobha, a strong, independent woman, traveled from Chicago to London and London to Delhi. She was very happy to be back and see her two small boys Ashiem and Ashish. Shobha was helped to get back safely by Vanita, who had lots of experience traveling by herself.

Certain things have been difficult to mention in this book, and we don't know how to write them. Thanks to our wonderful readers for understanding.

Shobha and Arun Berry

IT IS WORTH noticing that Shobha was a lucky person to come into all our lives.

To Arun, Shobha was the ultimate gift and soulmate. She was a great chef, amazing housekeeper, and loyal wife.

She would cook for many people—especially when Pradeep and Connie were set to go back to the US after a visit, which is when at least 20 people would drop in to say goodbye to them. They would often stay for dinner and drink whiskey, scotch or sodas.

Shobha and Her kitchen

SHOBHA WOULD KEEP herself extremely busy in the kitchen, cooking dishes. Our home in Bali Nagar was where people would meet or see Pradeep and Connie whenever they were in India.

Now, all our family members are slowly dying, and Connie, Shobha, and Pappi are no longer with us physically. But spiritually, it is not easy to forget them.

Shobha and her Health

SHOBHA SUFFERED FROM vascular problems, which caused pain in her legs and even put her in depression. The problem increased when we were at our house in Bali Nagar and became worse after we moved to the three-story house in Rohini.

It was in that house where she breathed her last breath on November 8, 2018, at 6:45 p.m. All her family members, starting with her husband and sons, were shocked and affected negatively.

Shobha had had three vascular surgeries and one plastic surgery. Her demise was due to the weakness in her body, and despite being a woman with a strong will, her heart eventually gave out from the suffering.

Staying with Her Body

When Shobha died, Pradeep was immediately fly out to Delhi as he was in shock. But he was happy that our younger half-brother Vikram and his wife Monica were with Shobha's body the whole night until she was cremated in the morning.

Pradeep was very upset and could not immediately come to attend the funeral due to his problems, and only arrived on November 23, 2018, for the last rituals—solve, or 16 days prayers of peace. He stayed with the family for three months, as our sister Pappi was very much in shock and was very badly affected by Shobha's death.

Our Wonderful Sister's Views

After Connie died in 2015, Kiran would often ask Pradeep to move back to Delhi permanently, rather than living in the US alone in grief. And now, she has left us and gone.

Arun, the Classical Singer

ARUN, TRAINED IN music by Satish Bhatia, was very well known among his friends for his singing. However, he dropped all the happiness of music after the demise of Shobha.

Life is a Duty

REGARDLESS OF WHAT state our lives are in and our current thoughts, we will always miss these great women in our lives—Connie, Shobha, and Pappi. It's very difficult to get over these three demises, which happened within short spans of each other. We have seen many people dying, but these were very difficult losses to sustain.

It is important to mention that the motto of caring for humanity lived our lives—we have considered ourselves a strong family, with faith in God and others.

Life is a wonderful duty; it is our motive, and the most important part of our relationship with our wonderful wives has been our wonderful love.

We are Born with Purpose

WHY DO WE say that we're not happy in our lives and families?

It's because we don't even know what the purpose of our life and soul is. Our wonderful gift of God is to bless those suffering from depression, poverty, education, sickness, and are in troubled situations. We must be strong people to help others in this troublesome life, live for humanity, and ultimately succeed in our own lives. Tell your family and friends to help others, and realize that your purpose in life is attained with love.

Education is Wealth

ONE OF THE best things in life is **education**. Educated people are respected all over the world, and it has something to offer to the society we love and live in.

Education shows us how to make a career, which will grow and become a wonderful lifetime gift of God. The progress of humanity is in education.

Our wonderful family is a blessing for us—they are our strength and help overcome the weakness of death in this world of both happiness and suffering. Many thanks to our wonderful readers, who too are in our prayers and thoughts all the time. We wish them a great peaceful life.

Both Shobha and Connie were the eldest daughters-in-law of our family. It is not easy to ever forget them. We would heavily miss both of them and our sister Rita Berry/ Kiran Revri—no matter what.

PERENNIAL LOVE

Death and Face

SITTING IN EVANSTON and hearing about his sister-in-law Shobha's death on that fateful night—November 8, 2018—Pradeep asked his heartbroken brother Arun to show him her face through an online video as she lay. He wanted to see Shobha Berry one last time before she left for her heavenly abode.

Arun was reluctant, as Indian culture didn't allow for unveiling a deceased person's face. However, Pradeep persisted on seeing his bhabhi's face one last time, and Arun agreed, showing him Shobha's shining face as her body lay covered in white clothes, to be taken away to be washed and ritualized. Pradeep saw once more how a life partner had decided to undertake a spiritual journey alone to the Supreme Lord. No more breath, only body.

Does it mean that only breath is life? No breath, no life—if someone died, their hands, face, legs, hair, eyes, full body is not destroyed, except the breath, which is a wonderful life in the darkness of happiness and joy. With death, the immortal love is gone.

The soul goes onto a new life, which can't be destroyed or burnt in the fire of a cremation chamber. Pradeep had seen the burning body of his own life partner Connie in the US, who died in 2015.

Pradeep remembers how one night he and Shobha talked about their thoughts on life and the Lord. Some think of collecting and saving money in life for the future, but they agree that death can come anytime, and no one knows where and when. Our body is not our own body but merely a temporary phase of life, and its destruction is a must. Man is born alone and dies alone with empty hands. No one brings a penny with us when born, and no one will take a penny when death occurs—we take only our karma with us. So please, let us do all we can to accumulate good karmas. Hell and heaven is on this earth, and your own life is yours while you are living, today, June 25, 2020, is the marriage anniversary of Shobha and Arun. It is upsetting that Shobha could not be with him to make it to the golden jubilee of their marriage—her demise on November 8, 2018, voided this gap.

We must appreciate our existence, struggle with the darkness, and turn dreams into happiness and reality, all with passion and love. Happiness depends upon our minds and circumstances. Our love, our relationships, our happiness and joy, and the blessings of others live forever. Please don't hesitate to open your thoughts and prayers to express the passion of love and loss in life. We both often do the same to express the loss of our love—of Shobha, Connie, and Kiran.

Living with humanity and compassion is the best way to get back to our lives of happiness. Silence, self-respect, kindness, and self-determination should be our hallmarks. Express your wonderful thoughts for achieving humanity, which will only add endless dimensions to our souls and give us inner strength.

I must mention that on that flight from Delhi to Frankfurt on January 15, 1976, I was confused and homesick. While changing flights to go from Frankfurt to Chicago, I decided to get a return ticket. However, I didn't have enough money to buy a one-way ticket—I had only seven dollars.

The flight captain from Frankfurt to Chicago told me that I wouldn't be able to go back to Delhi immediately, as my ticket had restrictions that meant I had to stay a minimum of 14 days in Chicago—which meant the earliest I could go back was January 29. That was when I met Connie. He was kind enough to make a reservation for me for January 31 while I was stuck in between to wait it out.

Constance Ann Fuller was the young girl who brought into my life happiness and success. It was love at first sight, resulting in a secret marriage in a Chicago courtroom on January 28, 1976.

On the flight from Frankfurt to Chicago, I recalled when a friend decided to leave his family to Germany after leaving his family business. Within two weeks, he returned to Delhi and remained in hiding from his family and friends, who finally only realized he was back when he got out to see a movie with Arun.

It was very difficult to consider my own life if I returned as a failure halfway from the way to America. That is why I am glad that Connie came into my life for a story that lasted 46 years. How can life change? And that too this quickly?

It's a puzzle—we're not going to get to the bottom of the game, but we can do our best to win the game of this puzzling chessboard. A chessboard is a brainwashing game to play, but once you play, you can do it better and get to teach your own experience of life and draw your conclusions. But love is love, and it's a wonderful gift for loved ones—true love.

How can I keep enough faith to carry on the dreams in my mind and my heart? How do I overcome my negative thoughts? Can I put into action a simple, healthy strategy to get to know yourself, to find a purpose to discover your own life and happiness?

I want to know my purpose and discover my humanity and talents, my thoughts of humanity. I get motivational quotes from my wife and my family. My sister is in my thoughts and prayers. Her sacrifices cannot be repaid in our lives or through our karmas as her mother died, leaving her to give us our happiness and joy in her ways.

Pappi, we are missing you and your deeds, caring for us brothers Arun and Pradeep.

We believe our wives and sister brought us luck and gave us happiness and prosperity. Thank you, Shobha, Connie, and Kiran. In Arun's own words, Shobha brought good luck to him. Connie brought Pradeep the excellent gift of happiness and blessings to succeed in his life. Kiran too brought prosperity and happiness in the life of humanity

Relieve some stress for your family and children to better their lives and academic career life.

Why should we give pain and trouble to others? Purify your mind—be engrossed in the welfare of all human beings. We should have the feeling of service all the time, throughout our lives. We learned our lessons from our wives and sister.

Arun can't even think of listening to sad songs, as they remind him of Shobha. Pradeep, too listens to those songs and thinks of Connie. We get very emotional while thinking of our sister Kiran and her style of talking about her life and happiness, which often made us laugh. Kiran had a wonderful heart—she was fun to be with and would laugh and giggle.

Arun's first book is based upon the true story of his own life with his wife, Shobha. The two were married for 48 years. After such a long marriage, her death fell hard on Arun, especially when most people need more attention after retirement. The same thing is being experienced by Pradeep and Surinder, our late sister's husband.

Life is full of surprises. True and pure love—be it of your significant other, mother, father, or wife—is a double-edged sword that brings pain and joy. If you were never gifted that love, then you would not feel as much pain when someone passes; however, if you have been blessed with deep love, the downside is that the pain is much deeper after they are gone. According to Khalil Gibran, the Lebanese author, life, and death are "even as the river and the sea are one." He says to trust in your dreams, for in them is hidden the gate to eternity.

Lord Buddha has said that our bodies are given to us by our parents, nourished by food, and destroyed one day. Just like Shobha, Connie, and Kiran. Our three husbands remain to face the sadness.

On June 16, 2020, I went to 1543 North Wells Street, Old Town, Chicago, to visit and pay my tributes and love to Connie's late wife. On January 24, 1976, she met me at 5:45 p.m. at the Indian restaurant, Gateway to India at the above address. She was my first and last love, as I married her on January 28, 1976.

Constance Ann Fuller was the love of my life—a great love that lasted four decades until she died at 1:10 a.m. on February 28, 1976. It was a wonderful gift from God to my family and me to have a great, peaceful relationship with Connie, who was the reason behind my success in life, career, humanity, and a source of happiness throughout our life. Thanks to my wife for this gift of humanity and the courage to survive in my life.

There was a new renter in 1543, North Wells Street, Old Town, Chicago, and he showed me his apartment, where I had lived so many years ago with three chefs. It was a very difficult emotional experience that day. I signed a book which I gave to the owner for his help in showing me his apartment, where I had lived many years ago.

Later, I went to 1836, West Lincoln Park West in Old Town, Chicago, where Connie lived when I met her. We were very close, and we became life partners, immediately getting married four days after we met. She died on the night of February 27-28, 2015.

I saw the same apartment where I had stayed in Chicago for the first time after moving to the US and meeting my future wife, Connie. Thanks, Connie…

Darling of Millions is a wonderful gift to humanity written by Pradeep Berry, author of six books.

We have to remember that we are all debtors to the world, and the world does not owe us anything. It is a great privilege for all of us to be allowed to do anything for the world. In helping the world, we help ourselves.

A sincere man feels for the troubles and tribulations of others and tries his level best to alleviate their sufferings. He is very sympathetic, soft-hearted, and also generous. He is always reliable, quite frank, honest, and true. He is free from crookedness, hypocrisy, cheating, and double-dealing. People place implicit faith in his words.

—Swami Sivananda

It is very difficult for me to define Shobha's greatness and how she helped her family—apart from homely duties of serving freshly cooked food by her own hands. When Pradeep left for the US in 1976 via Lufthansa Airlines, she arranged an Ambassador Car, driven by her father's driver Ram. Shobha and her 1-year-old son dropped him at the airport at Palam—now Indira Gandhi International Airport (DEL).

When Connie and Pradeep came to Delhi in July 1979 for the first time after their love marriage, there were received by Arun, Shobha, and their young sons in their green color fiat carat the airport.

Shobha was the queen of the kitchen and a source of happiness for her sister-in-law Connie and brother-in-law Pradeep, as well as our other family members. Connie was the star of the family, along with Shobha and Kiran. It is very difficult for us to imagine that our three diamonds are no longer with us in physical life, except in a spiritual way.

Now, at Arun's house in Rohini, Arun and Ashiem live on the ground floor, while Ashish and his family—wife Mona and daughters Krishna and Radhika—live with them. This is also a source of happiness in our lives in lots of ways. How life can change in our lives can't be defined by our family members and us.

One evening, I noticed the question of my life that had come to an end. That evening was November 8, 2018, at 6,45 PM when I was in my room and my wife was in the room. I suddenly saw her last breath, and she was gone to heaven to my surprise. I noticed that on that evening only. Also, I kept thinking about the answer for my life? If it had come before in and out on my lips if something happens to my life partner Mrs. Shobha Berry.A mother of two boys, Mr. Ashiem Berry and Mr. Ashish Berry, a mother-in-law, Mr. Ashish Berry, and his wife, Mrs. Mona Berry, and our two granddaughters, Miss Krishana Berry and Miss Radhika Berry.

At the same time, I thought about my younger biological brother Pradeep Berry who has been in the USA since January 15, 1976. He, too, recently lost his life partner Mrs. Constance Ann Berry, Ph.D., MBA, Master, who was snatched from Pradeep Berry on February 28, 2015. Till it was not even in his mind, soul, and lips, A series of life memories were coming and going through my mind and Pradeep's mind.

We both were very happy to be married, not to forget our wife's gift of love, now what happened all of a sudden the sadness appeared on our face. Only those two days, we both noticed.

We both were very happy and had the pride to be with our wife. All sorrows were far away from our life. However, the same sorrow came into our lives and souls, including Pradeep Berry, who flew to Delhi from USA. to be with our family. Our wives were not far from us and the same sorrow. We tried to hide so much harder and walked so much to keep our happiness away from us in our life.

Our hearts were full of love which was taken away from us. Our pain came back to us in our life. It walked towards my life, and the life of Pradeep and the doomsday was in our life on those two days, until this day.

We truly noticed that on November 8. 2018, The suspended pain and the question of Pradeep life was in pain on February 28, 2015, was absolutely nothing but was a life of sorrows which was crushed and devastated was back to destroy had come back since December 1, 2021.

Happiness is defined as a gift from God and our own family, especially when you get married to your love. Shobha married Arun in 1972, after our sister Rita (Kiran) married Surinder Revri in 1969, following the death of our grandparents in mid-1969.

It was a very difficult time for our grandparents to digest the worries of Rita, as well as the death of her daughter's husband—our mother's younger sister Bholi Aunty's husband, whose untimely death was a very big shock to our grandparents. However, Shobha's arrival had a very soothing effect on the family and friends, and she brought great luck to us. Pradeep met his future wife in 1976 in Chicago, IL, US, which resulted in love at first sight and a secret marriage at the Chicago courthouse. It was the start of four decades of a lovely marriage.

Now, in July 2020, both brothers Arun and Pradeep are thinking about our wonderful life partners and our sister Kiran. This remembrance is a wonderful gift to our family and friends, especially a tribute to Shobha Berry, whose wonderful book is written in memory.

It's worth mentioning that Shobha was very hospitable to the elders. In our house in Bali Nagar, our parents and grandparents often visited and stayed with Arun and

Shobha, as did Connie and Pradeep when they came to India.

Shobha's life was loaded with cooking day and night—one single soul was cooking for our entire family and friends and anyone who would drop by, no matter what! But we never realized that she stood for hours and hours on end without thinking of anything else—we ask forgiveness for our ignorance and happiness because our happiness was her unhappiness. We did not realize this until many years later. Shobha, please forgive your brother Pradeep and husband Arun. Hopefully, Shobha will forgive us.

We are thinking of these things because her passion led to her sickness—Shobha suffered from vascular problems and pain. But she persisted without complaining as she wanted to control her kitchen, which she liked so much. But this most likely contributed to her vascular problems and painful legs, which led to swelling in her legs. We heard her cries due to her leg pain, but she kept going back and forth to and from the kitchen to serve her family and friends. Now her demise only leaves her great memories of hospitality.

We must admit our regret and appreciation for Shobha's dedication, and we truly ask her forgiveness for our ignorance. She knew everything in her kitchen, cupboard, wardrobe, bedroom, living room, and everything else in the house. She was the one who locked all the main doors in the house at night and unlocked them in the morning, almost like a trained watchman!

Nowadays, the watchmen are our family members, who take good care of the house and household work out of respect for our Shobha's memory.

Arun is extremely grateful to God for the blessings of his Shobha, who was unmindful of wealth or poverty in their married life. She appreciated what she had and was very happy with her husband, children, granddaughters, and extended family. We have all made do with what we got. Some of the other family members had been very unhappy with their property distribution and inheritance, which caused unhappiness. But we never had to fight for money and a comfortable living—because, with these wonderful women, we were in a comfort zone of happiness.

Lord bless their souls, wherever they are.

It's very difficult to find a ray of hope in our lives after the death of these wonderful women—we are doing our best to be happy with what we have now.

"No work, no food" was the wonderful ideological gift of the father of the nation, Mahatma Gandhi. His message was his life, or rather, his life was his message. We took this to heart and accomplished success. It provides us with a way of living through the current crisis.

Our minds keep thinking of Kiran Revri and her children—son Rajesh, his wife Pooja and son Bonnie;

daughter, Priya Makkar, her husband Raju Makkar, and their children Kashika and Mrinal.

We can talk or write about our wives all day long, without any hesitation. We are focused on writing down our thoughts and prayers for our wives' memory—no matter the opinion of gossips, critics, and well-wishers.

Love is our morning, afternoon, and evening. We must remember our happiness, gleaned from our life partners, with our wives for decades. We lost beautiful gifts from our lives, but we know that we can't do anything about it. We must explain and express our love in its purest and sincerest form to others who are not in love or don't know what love is.

The essence of our love is not about looking to solve the personal puzzles for others but rather to inspire others to solve their problems positively. We demonstrate our love by reflecting on the ways humanity and others can seek absolute wellness. Our main goal is to make our passion and love selfless for the good of all.

Our love should become a source of energy, passion, and inspiration for others—we hope to inspire this by sharing the unforgettable thoughts of life we have had with our partners. Dispel the desire for the things that cannot enrich our life with happiness and prosperity. It will be a great gift to the society we live in. Fighting and arguing are and against each other's nature. Love can change our culture, lives, depression, sadness—it can give us our ways of finding positivity in life through unforgettable experiences.

Let's not forget about the wonderful qualities of this four-letter word—LOVE, which is an evergreen gift of God.

Love is the morning, afternoon, evening, and night. Love is so strong that no matter what is going on in our lives, it can solve problems and stop enmity. It energizes us and inspires others to love and live their dreams, through which they may come to know themselves.

Love can explain our purpose, short and long-term dreams in life and drive us in our career and talents. Love, and spread love.

This book is our wonderful tribute to our wonderful wives and sister—the three great loves of our lives.

PERENNIAL LOVE

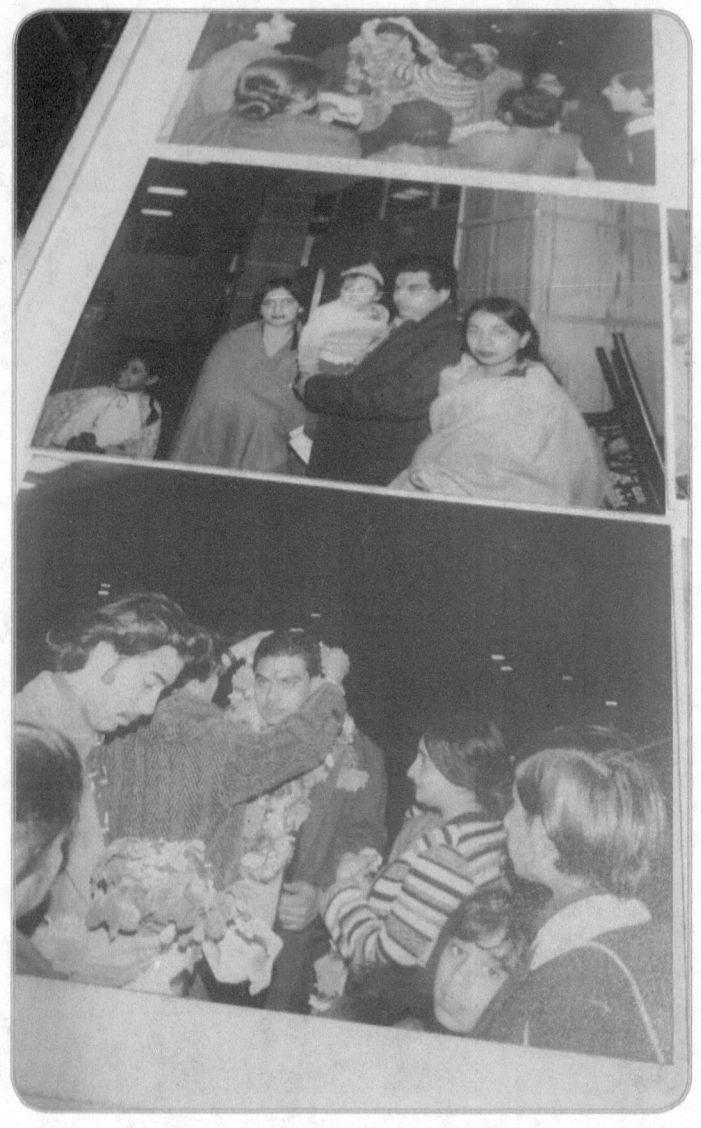

PERENNIAL LOVE

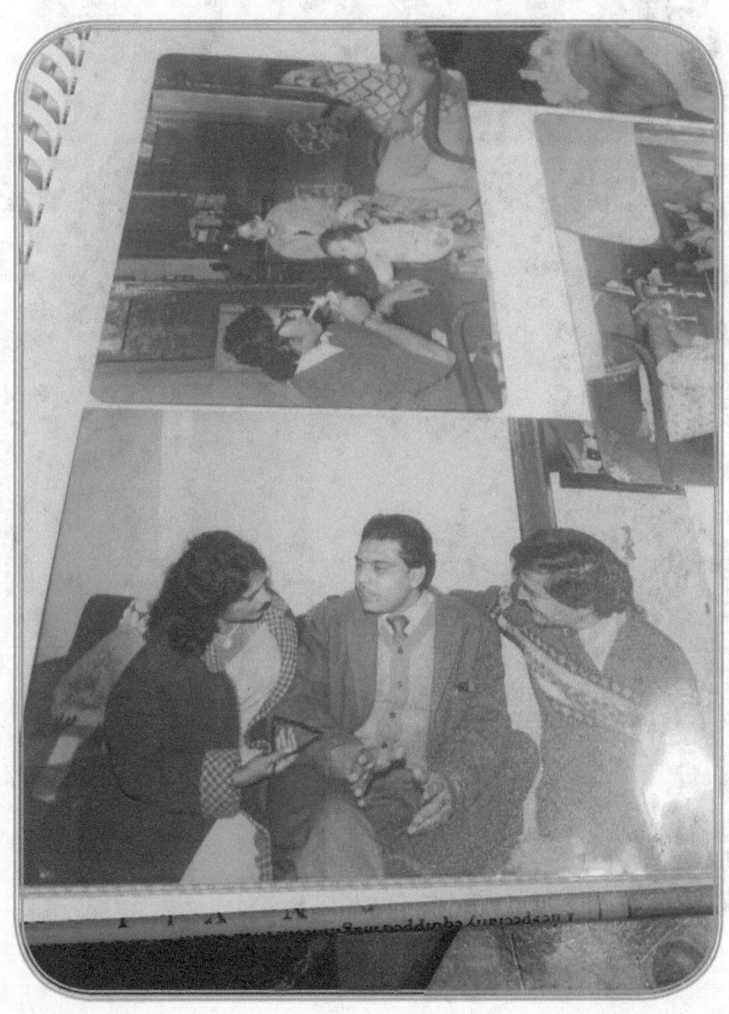

www.ingramcontent.com/pod-product-compliance
Lightning Source LLC
Chambersburg PA
CBHW012100090526
44592CB00017B/2641